Keyboard Chords
IN COLOR

Order No. AM 982014 ISBN-10: 0.8256.3358.3 ISBN-13: 978.0.8256.3358.4

Exclusive Distributors:
Music Sales Corporation 257 Park Avenue South, New York, NY 10010 USA
Music Sales Limited 14-15 Berners Street, London W1T 3LJ England
Music Sales Pty. Limited 120 Rothschild Street, Rosebery, Sydney, NSW 2018, Australia

Printed in the United States of America by Vicks Lithograph and Printing Corporation

Amsco Publications
A Part of **The Music Sales Group**
New York/London/Paris/Sydney/Copenhagen/Berlin/Tokyo/Madrid

table of contents

The diagrams used to illustrate the chords are very easy to read. The 3-D graphic shows the keys that make up the chord. The keys are pushed down for both the white and black keys, and shaded in light gray for the black keys. The notes of each chord are located below and above each note. The root of each chord is enclosed in a circle.

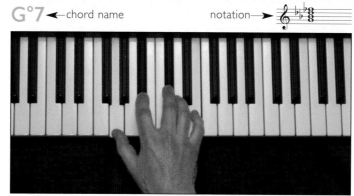

G°7 ←chord name   notation→

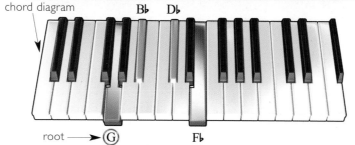

chord diagram

B♭   D♭

root → Ⓖ   F♭

Keyboard Chords in Color groups chords in a new way that makes looking up and learning new chords easier for you. The chords are grouped by family, so the chords you're likely to find together in any one piece are next to each other in the book. You can understand how they are related at a glance.

The photographs clearly indicate the suggested fingering for each chord. There is also an extra section on auxiliary chords.

C major

C major7

Csus4

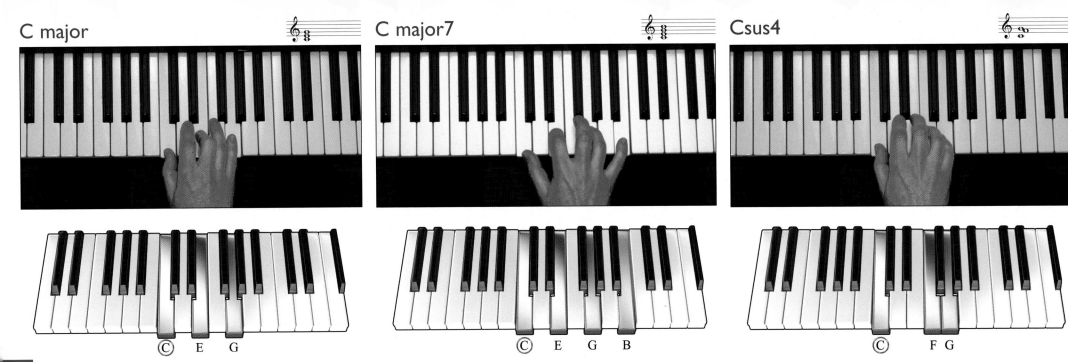

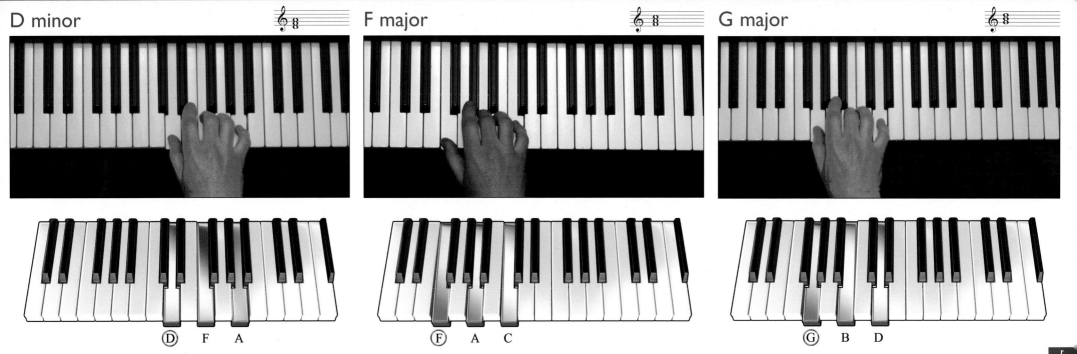

D minor

F major

G major

D F A

F A C

G B D

5

A minor

A minor6

A minor7

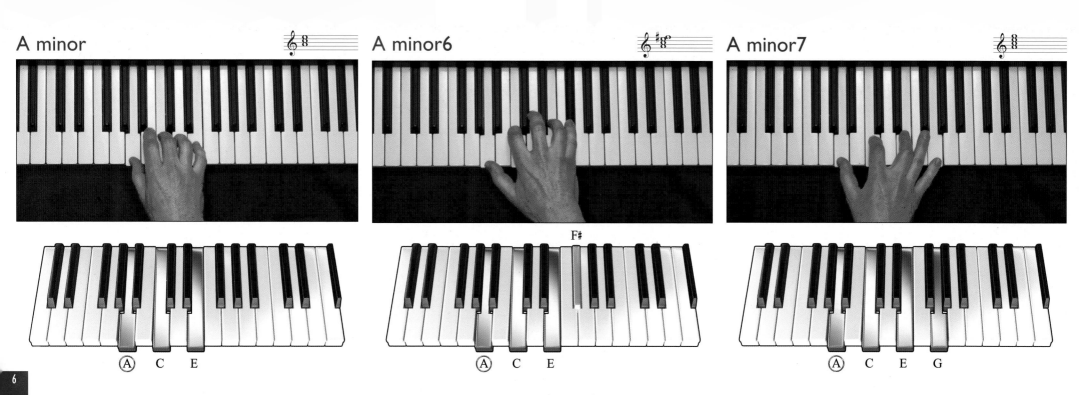

A minor — A C E

A minor6 — A C E F#

A minor7 — A C E G

6

D minor

E major

E7

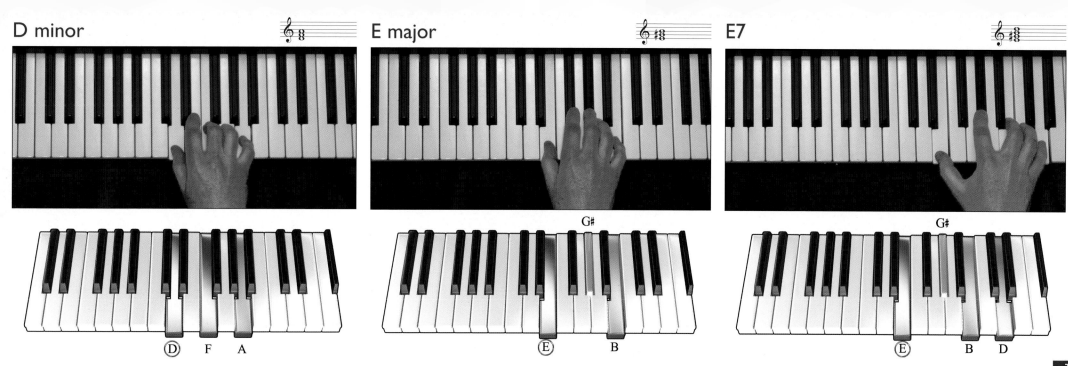

D minor: D F A

E major: E G# B

E7: E G# B D

G major

G major7

Gsus4

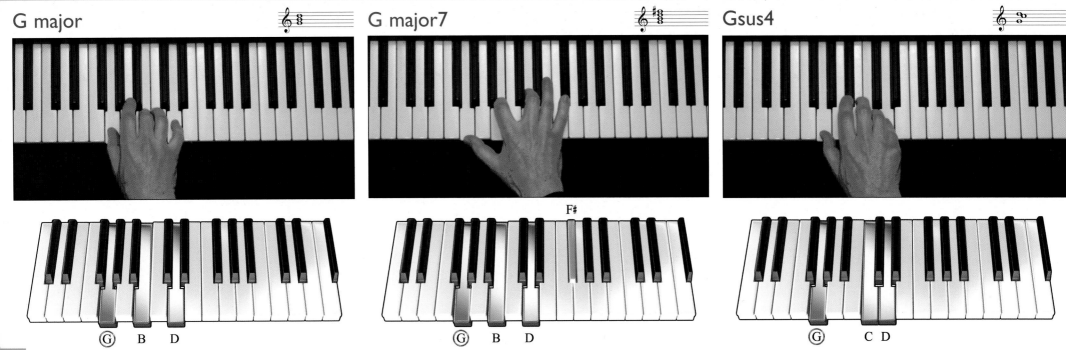

A minor   # C major   # D major

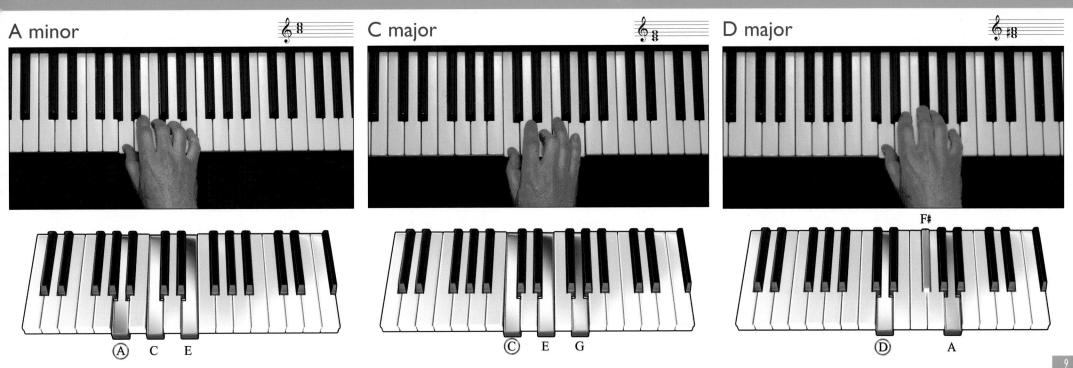

E minor

E minor6

E minor7

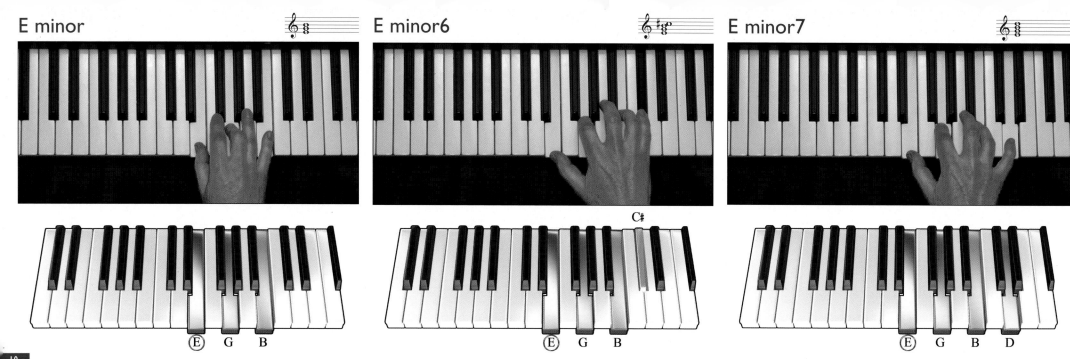

E minor: E G B
E minor6: E G B C#
E minor7: E G B D

10

A minor

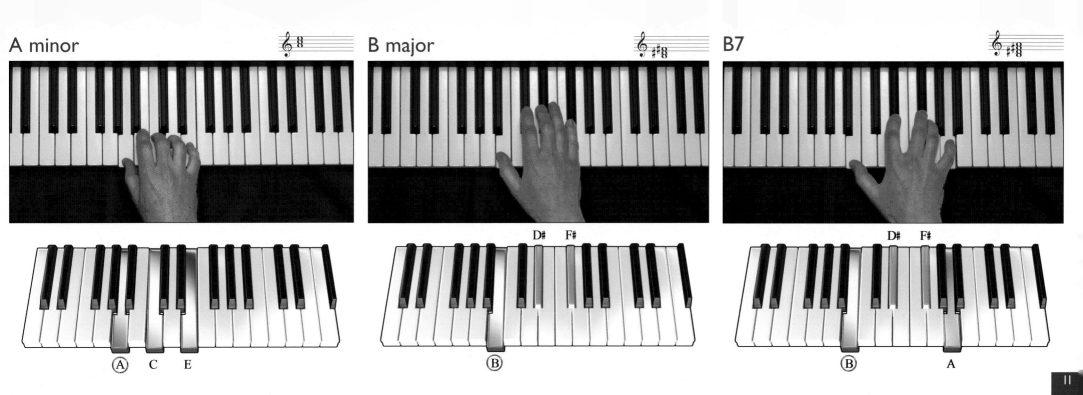

A C E

B major

D# F#

B

B7

D# F#

B A

D major

D major7

Dsus4

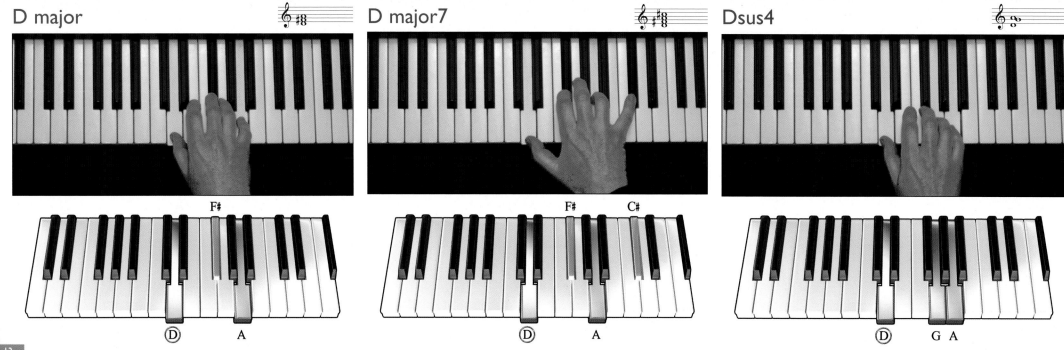

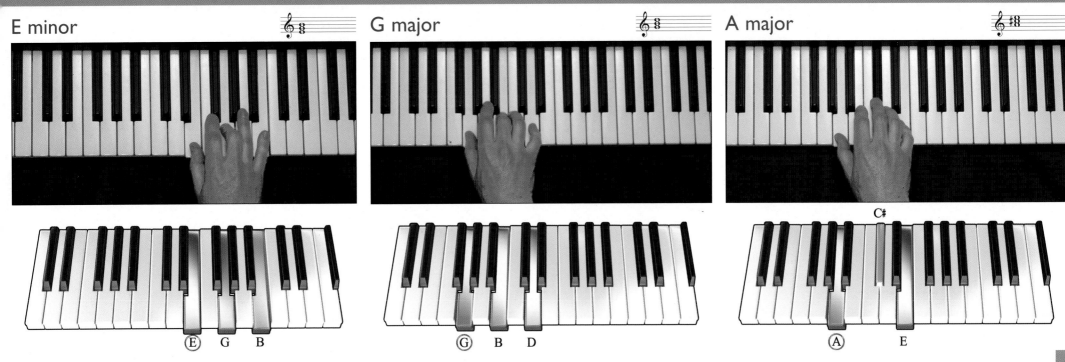

E minor

G major

A major

B minor

B minor6

B minor7

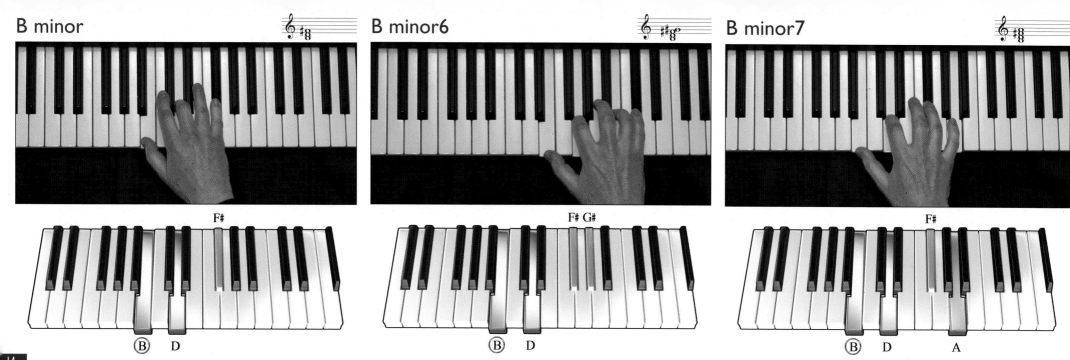

F#

F# G#

F#

Ⓑ D

Ⓑ D

Ⓑ D A

E minor

F# major

F#7

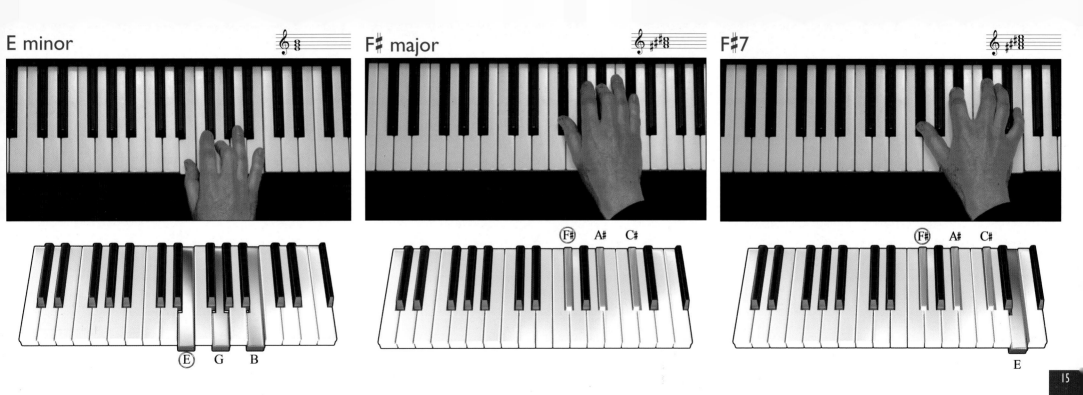

E   G   B

F#   A#   C#

F#   A#   C#

E

15

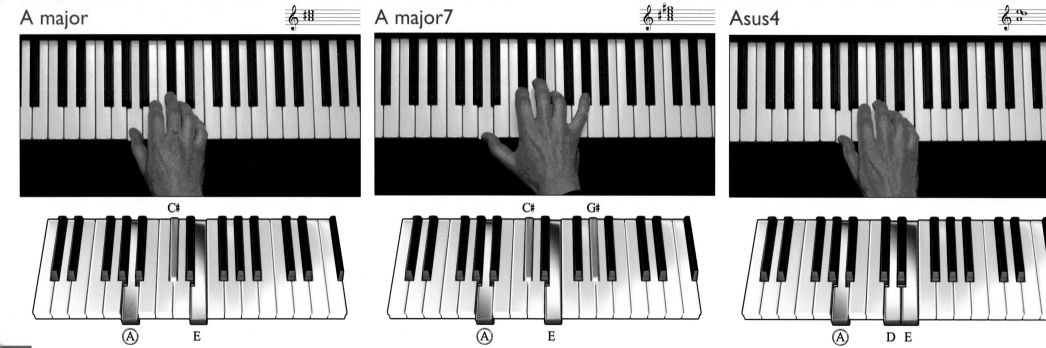

A major

A major7

Asus4

B minor

D major

E major

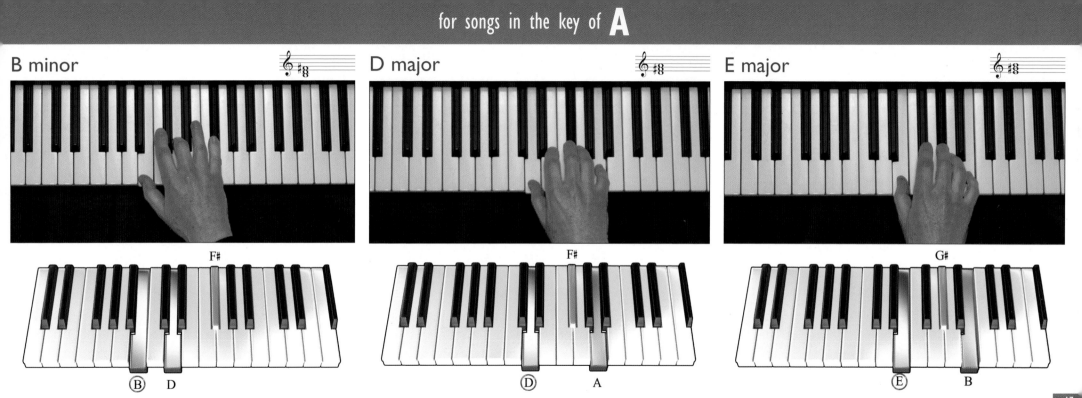

F#

F#

G#

Ⓑ D

Ⓓ A

Ⓔ B

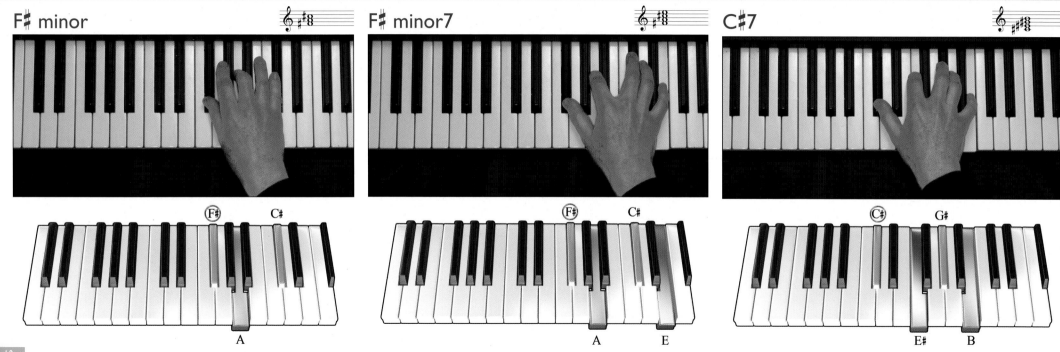

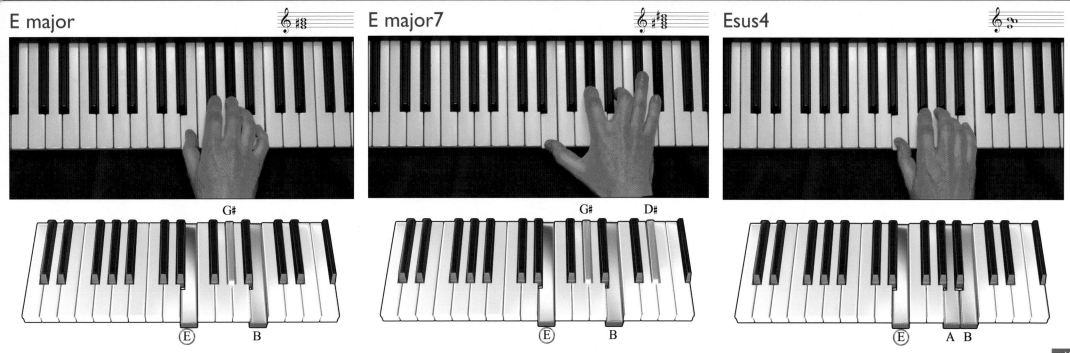

for songs in the key of **E**

E major

E major7

Esus4

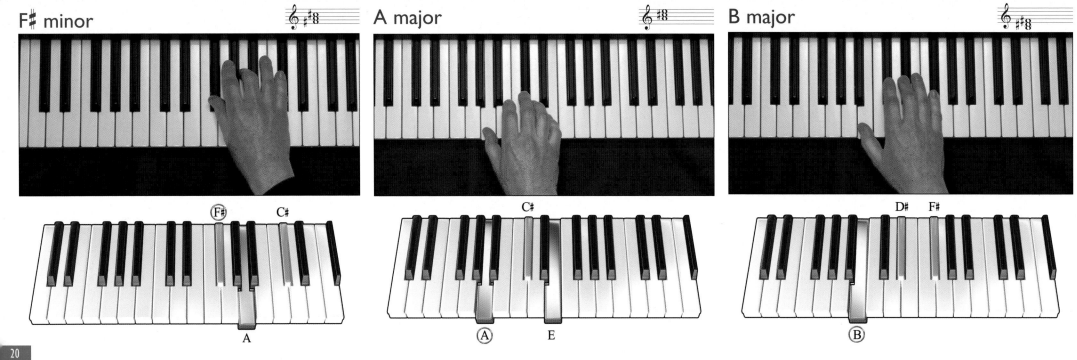

F# minor

A major

B major

C# minor

C# minor7

G#7

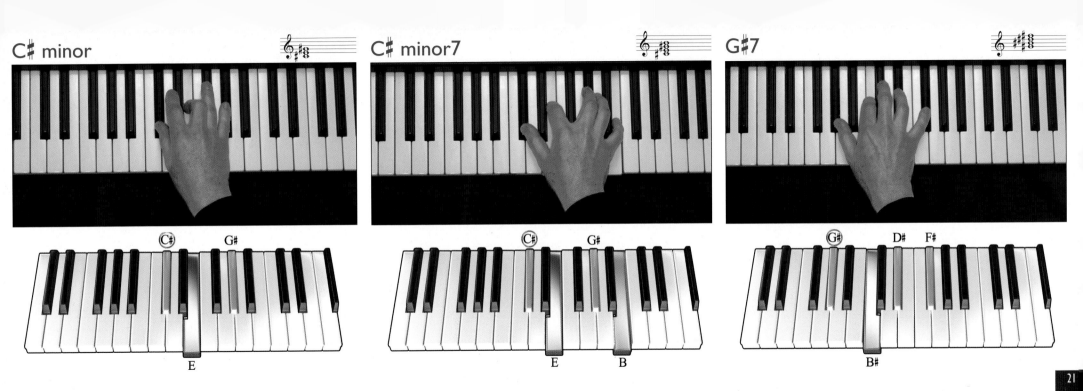

B major

E major

F# major

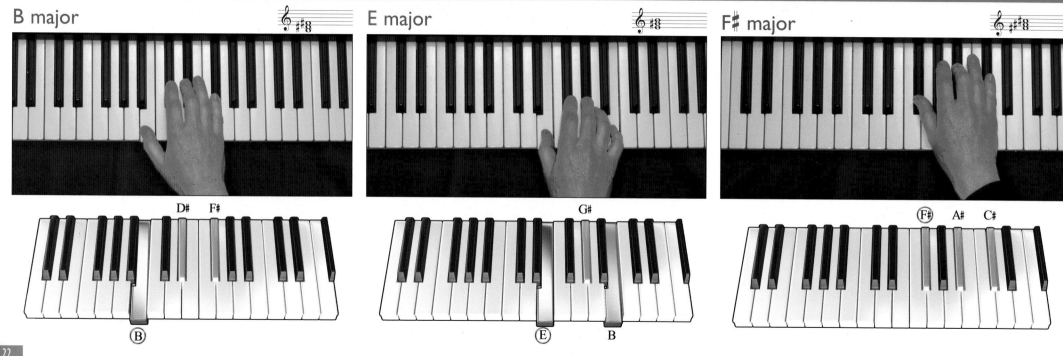

G♯ minor

G♯ minor7

D♯7

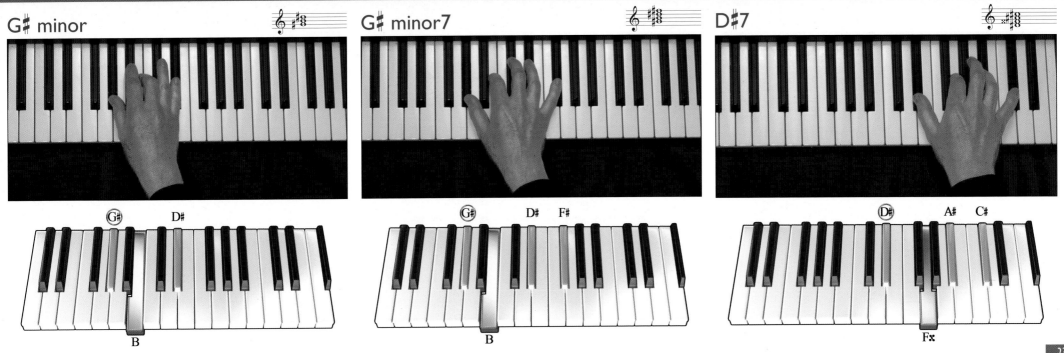

F♯ major

B major

C♯ major

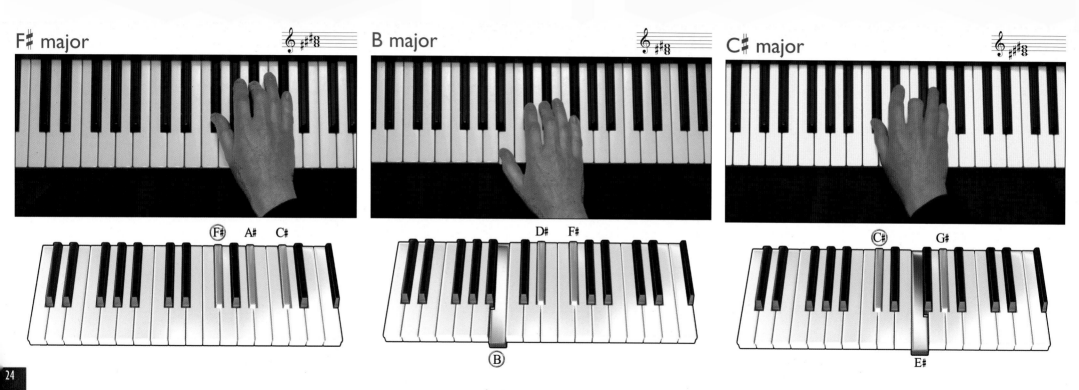

F♯ A♯ C♯

D♯ F♯

C♯ G♯

B

E♯

D♯ minor

D♯ minor7

A♯7

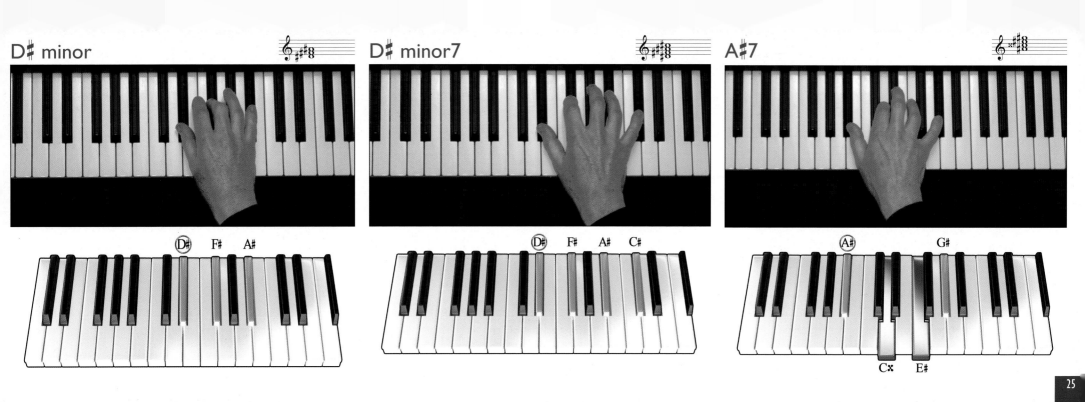

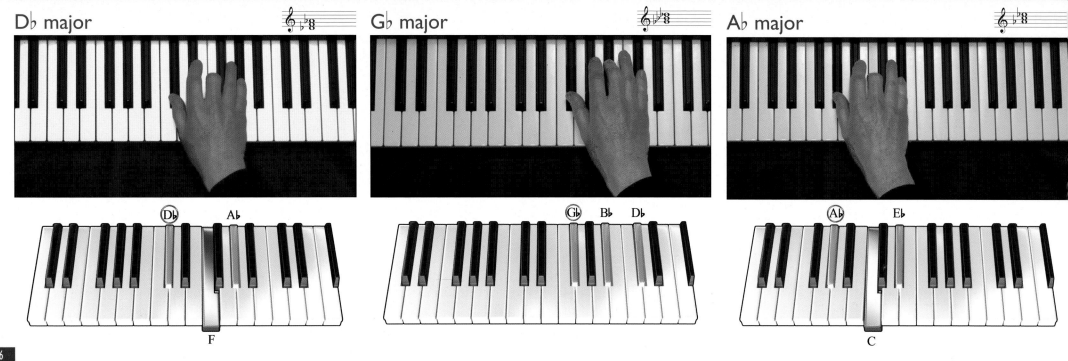

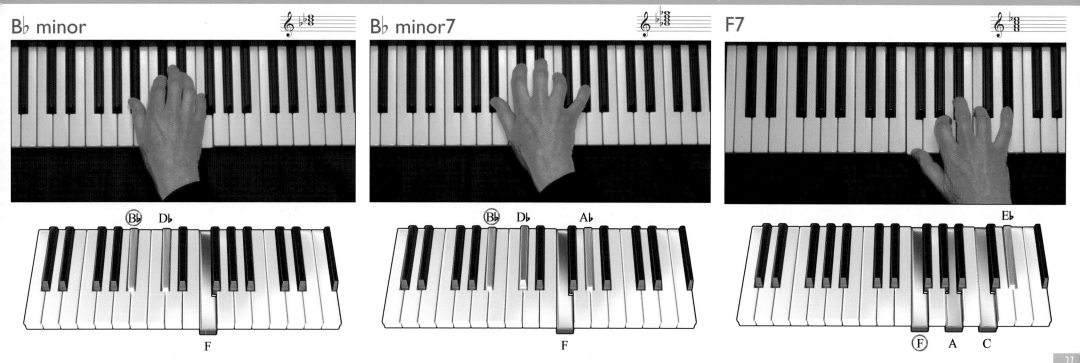

B♭ minor

B♭ minor7

F7

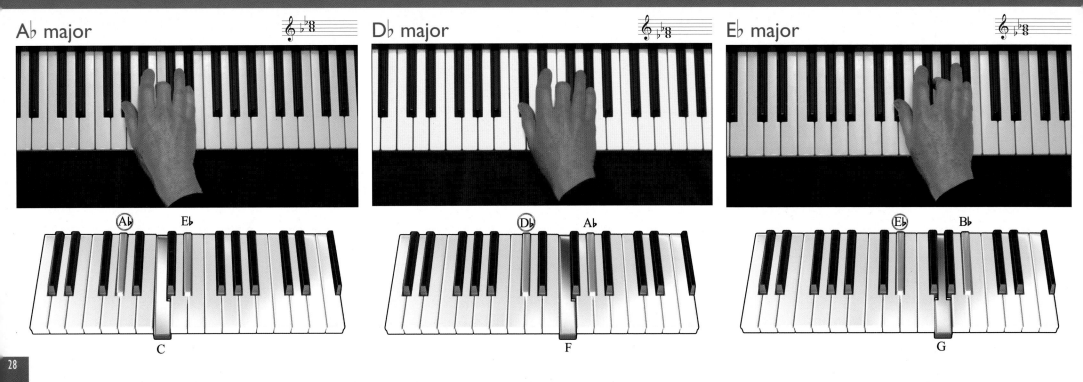

A♭ major

D♭ major

E♭ major

F minor

F minor7

C7

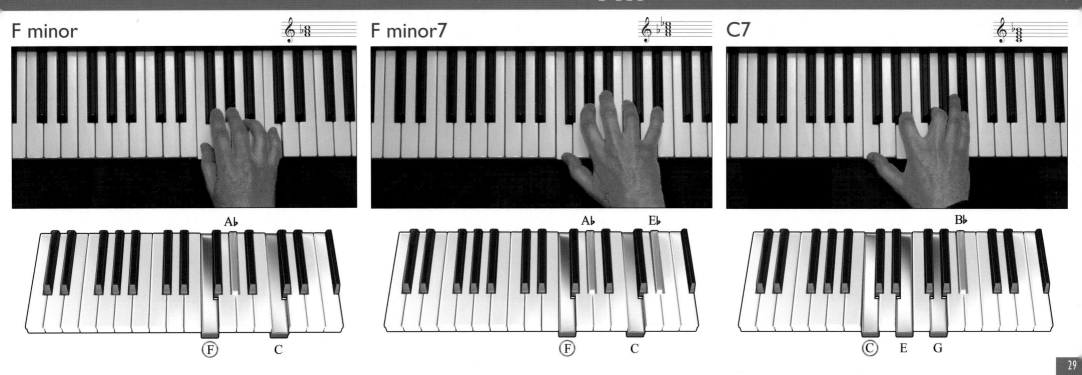

Ab

Ab   Eb

Bb

Ⓕ   C

Ⓕ   C

Ⓒ   E   G

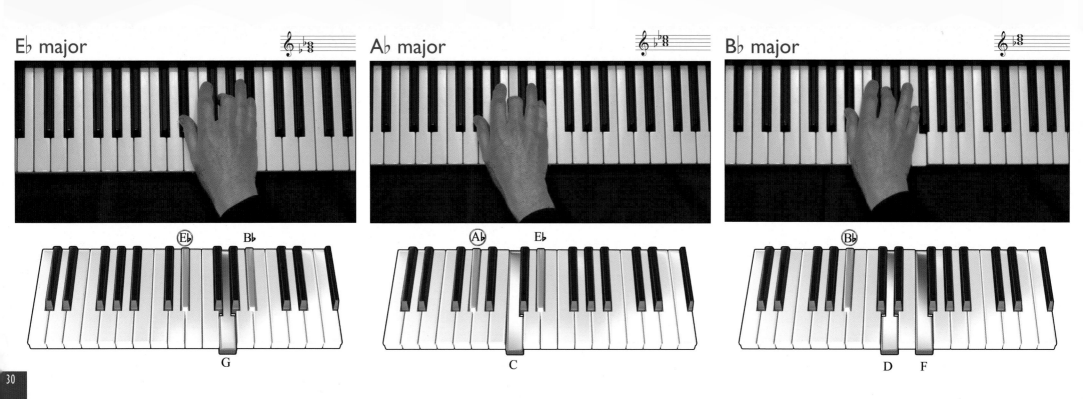

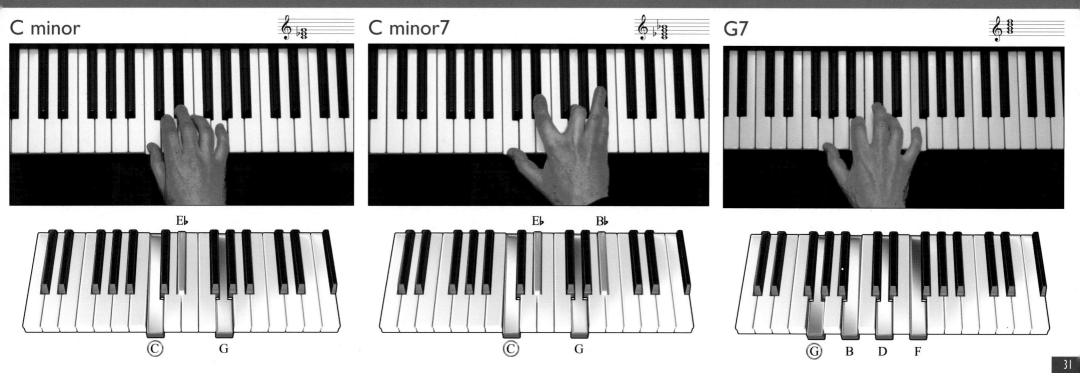

C minor

C minor7

G7

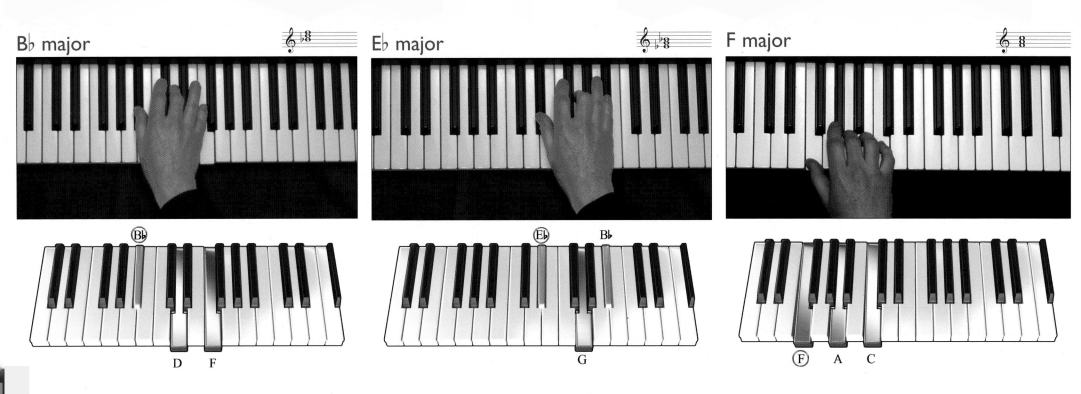

G minor

G minor7

D7

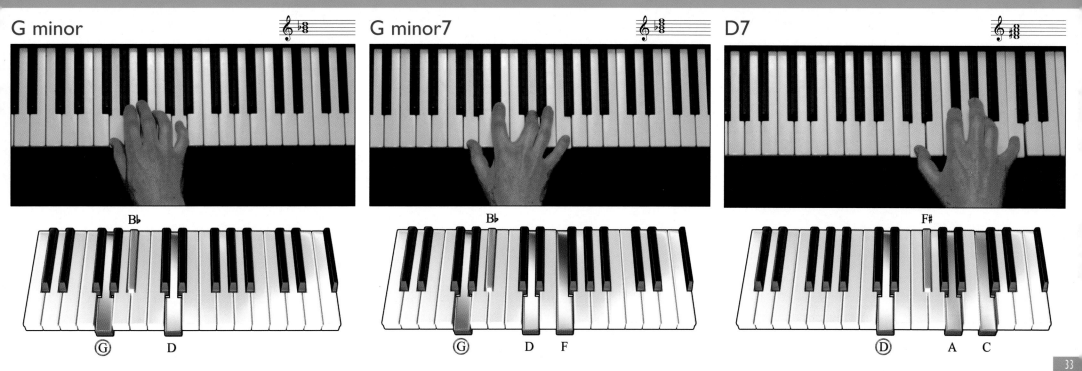

F major

B♭ major

C major

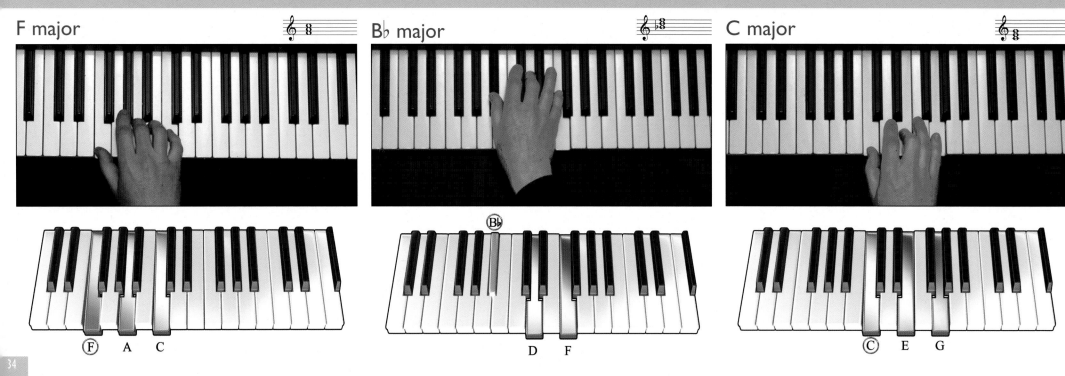

F   A   C

B♭

D   F

C   E   G

D minor

D minor7

A7

C augmented

C°7

C minor7♭5

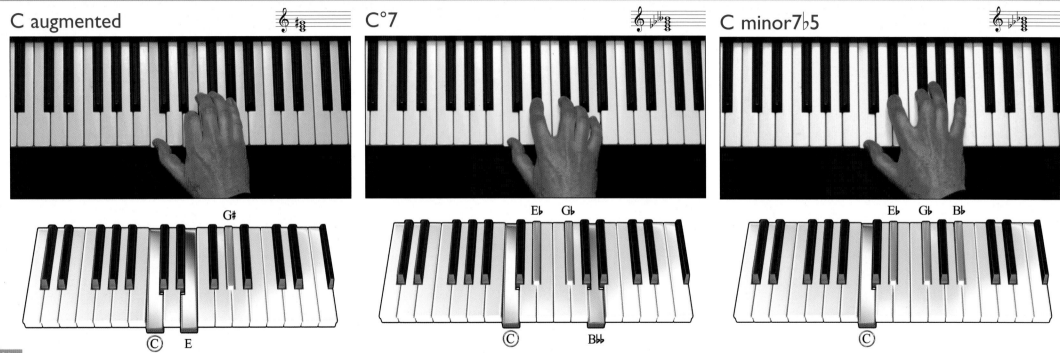

D♭ augmented

D♭°7

D♭ minor7♭5

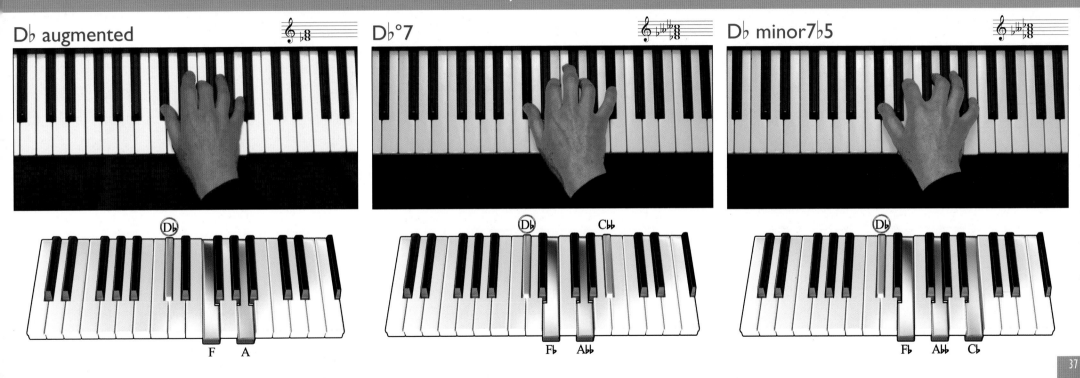

D♭ F A

D♭ C♭♭ F♭ A♭♭

D♭ F♭ A♭♭ C♭

D augmented

D°7

D minor7♭5

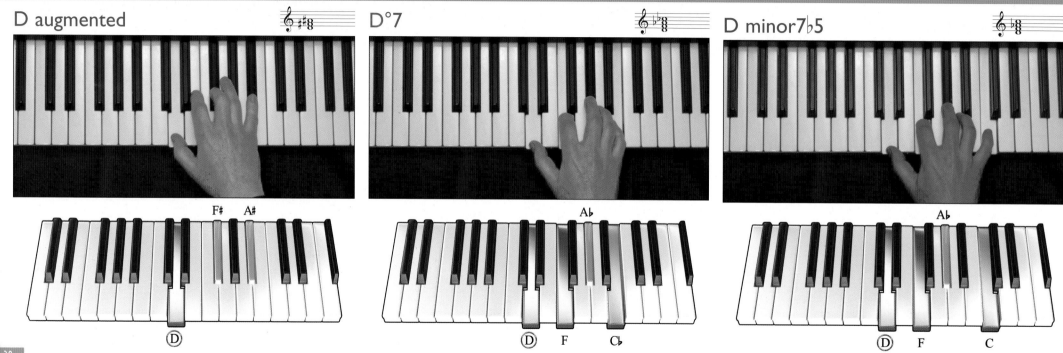

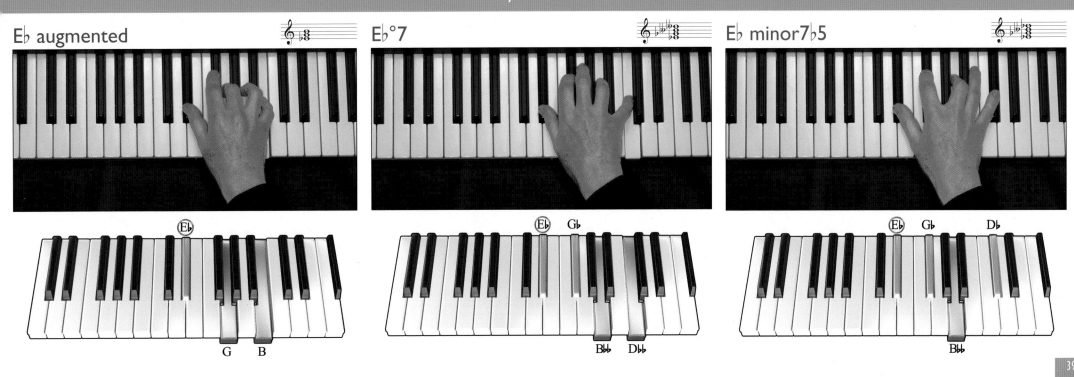

E♭ augmented

E♭°7

E♭ minor7♭5

E augmented

E°7

E minor7♭5

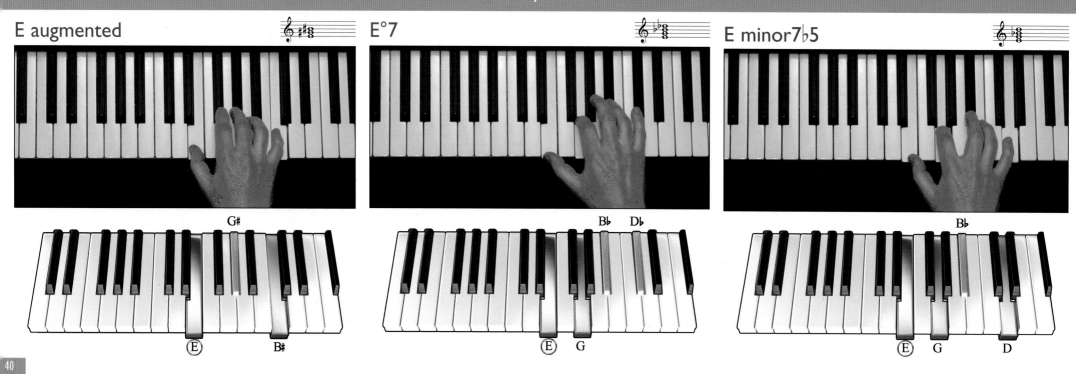

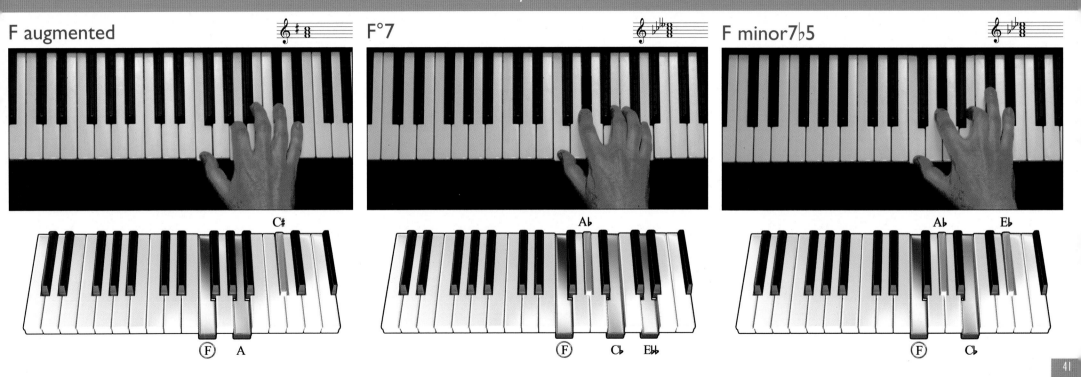

F augmented

F°7

F minor7♭5

C♯

F A

A♭

F C♭ E♭♭

A♭   E♭

F C♭

F♯ augmented

F♯°7

F♯ minor7♭5

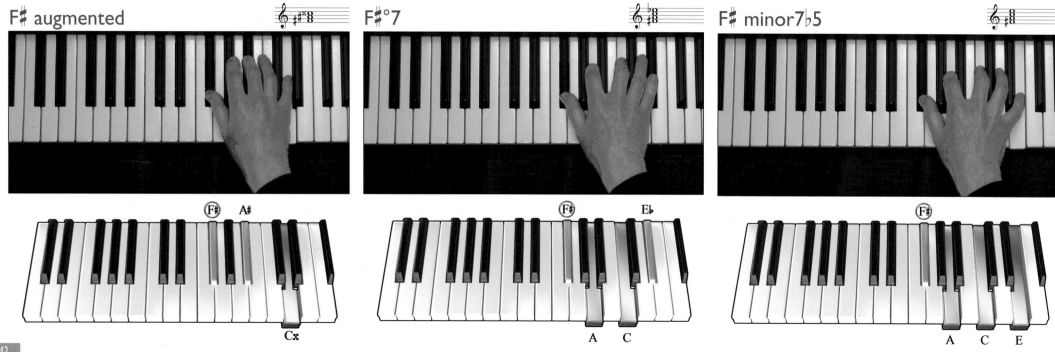

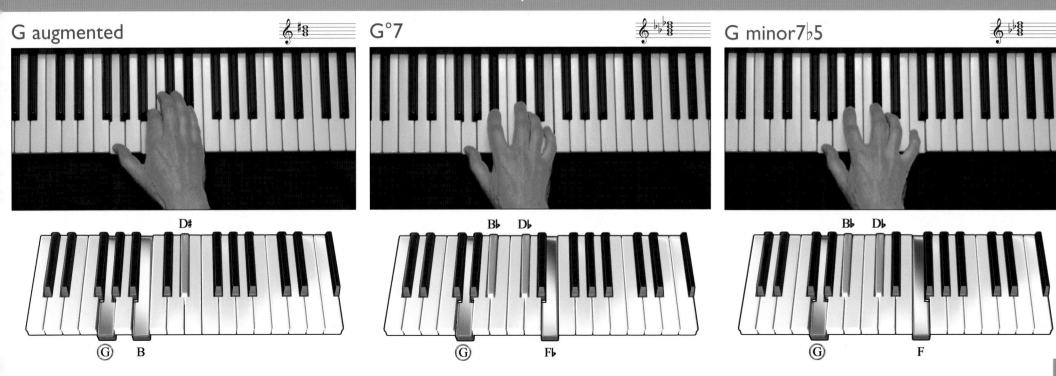

G augmented

G°7

G minor7♭5

D♯

G   B

B♭   D♭

G   F♭

B♭   D♭

G   F

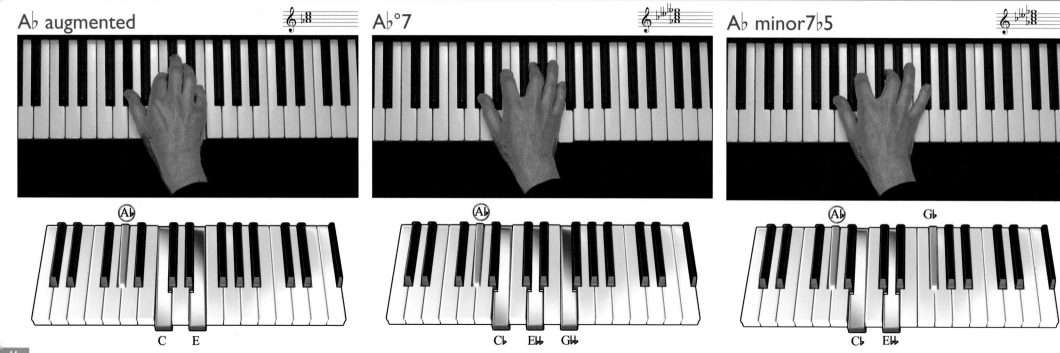

A♭ augmented

A♭°7

A♭ minor7♭5

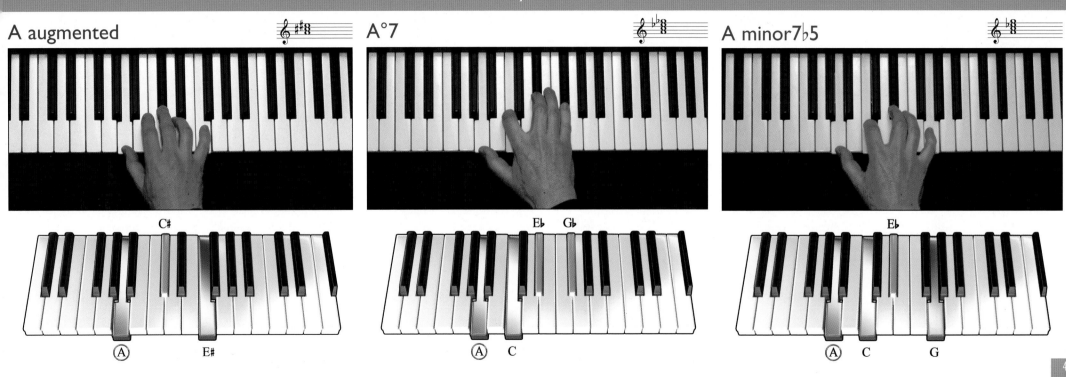

A augmented

A°7

A minor7♭5

C#

A

E#

E♭   G♭

A   C

E♭

A   C   G

45

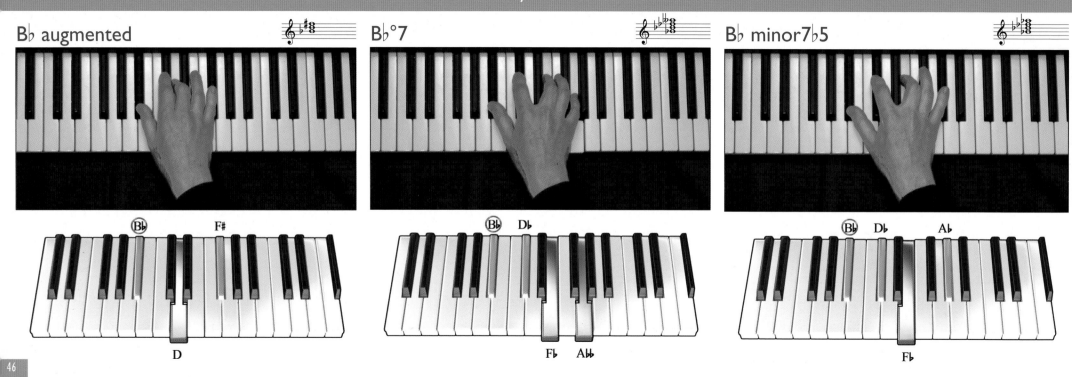

B♭ augmented

B♭°7

B♭ minor7♭5

46

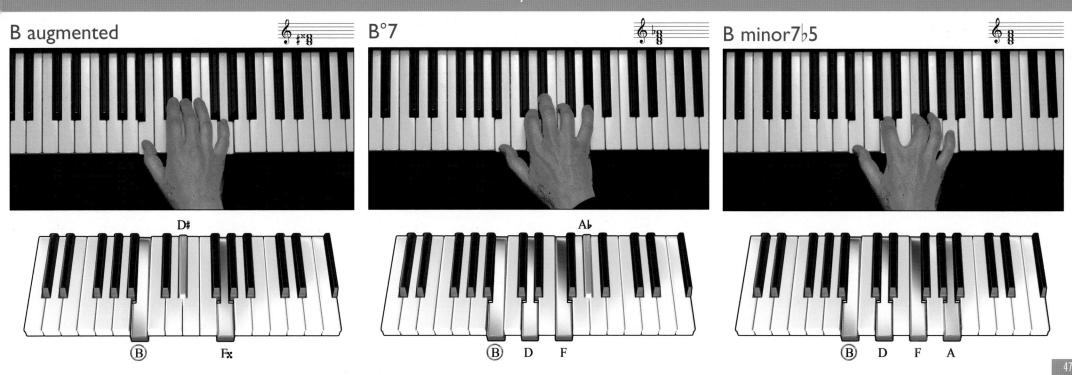

B augmented

B°7

B minor7♭5

Symbols used in this book	Chord Name	Alternate Symbols
Maj	Major	M; Major
m	minor	min; —
6	Major Sixth	Maj6; M6
m6	minor sixth	min6; —6
6/9	six-nine	6(add9); Maj6(add9); M6(add9)
maj7	Major seventh	M7; Maj7; Δ
7	dominant seventh	
m7	minor seventh	min7; —7
m(maj7)	minor with Major seventh	m(maj7); min(Maj7); m(+7); —(M7); min(add M7)
m7♭5	half-diminished seventh	½ dim; ½ dim7; ᵒ7; m7(—5)
ᵒ7	diminished seventh	ᵒ; dim; dim7
7+	augmented seventh	+7; 7(♯5); 7(+5)
7♭5	dominant seventh with flat(ted) fifth	7(—5)

Symbols used in this book	Chord Name	Alternate Symbols
9	dominant ninth	7(add9)
maj9	Major ninth	maj9; (Δadd9); Maj7(add9);M7(add9)
7♭9	dominant flat(ted) ninth	7(add♭9); 7—9; —9
m11	minor eleventh	min11; min7(add11); m7(add11)
maj7♯11	Major seventh with sharped eleventh	(+11); (Δ+11); M7(+11); (Δ♯11); M7(♯11)
13	dominant thirteenth	7(add13); 7(add6)
maj13	Major thirteenth	(Δadd13); Maj7(add13); M7(add13); M7(add6)
m13	minor thirteenth	—13; min7(add13); m7(add13); —7(add13); m7(add6)
sus4	suspended fourth	(sus4)
+	augmented	aug; (♯5); +5

enharmonic equivalents

A♯ = B♭

B = C♭

B♯ = C

C♯ = D♭

D♯ = E♭

E = F♭

E♯ = F

F♯ = G♭

G♯ = A♭

48